Get Rid of Anxiety & Panic Attacks
Guide For Teenagers and Young Adults
By Tilly McIntyre

Table of Contents

Introduction – Age 34

At the age of 17, I started to feel unwell. I constantly felt sick and just wanted to be at home all the time. I went to the doctors on numerous occasions and finally, when I took my mum with me, the doctor told me I had depression and anxiety. He explained to me the reason I was feeling sick was because I was anxious. The doctor gave me some anti-depressants and some anti-anxiety tablets. I felt nervous about taking the tablets, but took them as I desperately wanted to feel well again.

It was a really tough time for me. My friends were doing their A-Levels and planning their university placements and I was stuck at home with nothing going on in my life. I had always wanted a career and presumed that I would be going to university, but I just didn't feel well enough.

I was referred to counselling. Some of my sessions were funded by the NHS but I remember most of the sessions were funded by my parents. Looking back I don't know how they afforded this as we really didn't have the money. I also started having acupuncture for my anxiety which helped me loads. Over time I began to feel less and less anxious. Eventually I didn't feel anxious at all. However, I still felt sick.

I went back to my doctors and said that I no longer felt anxious, but I still felt sick. The doctor ran some tests and it turned out that I had a stomach bug called Helicobacter Pylori, which causes stomach ulcers. That was why I had been feeling sick all this time!

After the treatment I felt much better. I started working part-time in a school as a classroom assistant and started a degree in Psychology with the Open University. Studying with the Open University meant I could study at home and still progress in my career like I wanted to. It actually meant that I paid for my course each year and had no living expenses because I was living at home with my mum (I completed my degree with no student debt). The degree helped me to get various full time posts such as a social work assistant in a medium secure unit and then as a counsellor.

I completed my psychology degree after 6 years. I decided to go to London and do a Masters degree in Business Psychology. When I was feeling ill I could never have imagined that I would be commuting to London to study for a Masters degree. After this I set up my own training and coaching company and have been running this for 7 years. I would have never have thought any of this was possible when I was younger and suffering with anxiety.

I wrote this book when I was 21 years old after recovering from my anxiety. It was published shortly afterwards thanks to funding from UnLtd, National Lottery. Unfortunately the publishers went bankrupt shortly afterwards. This year I found the manuscript and decided to self-publish it on Amazon. I have left the manuscript as it was, just tidying it up here and there to make sure it makes sense. I wanted to keep it written by a young adult for teenagers and young adults. The introduction that follows is the introduction I wrote when I was 21 years old.

Introduction – Age 21

The thing to remember when recovering from anxiety is that it can take some time.

To beat anxiety you need a great deal of determination and courage. At times you may temporarily give up and think 'What's the point? This is useless!' At other times you may cry with pure frustration.

You must persevere. Take it step by step, day by day and eventually one day you will look back and realise just how far you have come.

NEVER give up on your fight for your health! Once you are well, life becomes so much easier. You may feel like you'll be like this forever but one day your suffering will disappear.

Follow the tips in this book. Re-read it many times and it will become your way of thinking. Thoughts control the physical sensations we feel. If we improve our thinking patterns we can improve how we physically feel.

Panic Attacks

Panic attacks are terrifying. They are surges of panic that make you feel absolutely awful.

Why Me?

Why you? Why anyone? You might think 'It's not fair. Why can't I be like that person walking down the street? Why aren't they anxious?' It seems unreal you used to be like them and walking around without a care in the world.

At least 1 in 10 people experience occasional panic attacks. There is no particular type of person that gets it. It can affect anyone, anywhere, anytime and at any age. You are not unique in that respect. There are thousands of people just like you who are suffering with anxiety every day. They do not look any different to anyone else. You may be in the supermarket and think 'Why is no one else feeling like this?' Chances are there is someone very near feeling like you or at least has felt like you. They do not have a flashing red light on their foreheads. You cannot tell. Don't believe me? Recall the last time you were in a busy place, the city, a shop, a park. Did you notice an anxious person? You probably didn't. You have seen thousands in your time, some even having panic attacks.

There are many people in the world who experience exactly what you do.

Causes

There is a big debate as to what causes anxiety. If you have a counsellor sometimes they will look at what contributed to your anxiety. However, sometimes there may be no cause. Possible causes might be:

Childhood Causes - An experience that seriously upset you or affected you. As you were young, you did not have the resources that you do now in order to deal with it properly. It may be directly linked to any fears or phobias that you have now. You may experience flash backs. I used to have a phobia of being sick. This apparently related back to when I was 3 years old and had whooping cough. I would run around the lounge on my tiptoes trying to catch my breath before I was eventually sick.

Severe Stress – Severe stress can make you feel on edge and anxious. It could be that you are experiencing a prolonged stressful situation over many months. For example, perhaps you are extremely stressed or worried about work. The thought of going to work may fill you with dread and you start to feel anxious. You then start fearing the anxious feelings you have. This can create a viscous cycle to the point where you start to feel anxious in other areas of your life.

Illness – Perhaps you have an illness which means that you experience certain symptoms. You might feel capable of managing the symptoms whilst at home, but find it difficult to manage the symptoms when out. Perhaps you have been housebound for a while and going outside now seems weird and daunting.

Inherited – It is thought that panic disorders may be passed down through the genes. If a close relative suffers with anxiety, the individual may be at an increased risk.

Trauma – Sometimes a traumatic event such as bereavement can cause a person to start having anxiety attacks. The anxiety might start straight away or it can be delayed and appear years later.

It is very important that you speak to your GP regarding your anxiety, if you have not already done so. Panic attacks can be caused by some medical conditions.

Panic attacks can be extremely unpleasant. You may experience a variety of different physical sensations. Panic attacks usually only last a few minutes and do not actually harm you. You will have probably experienced some or all of the following during anxiety or a panic attack:

Dizzy, disorientated, light headed, feint, blurred vision, difficulty in swallowing, tense body, heart racing, palpitations, shaky legs, sweating, shivering, wanting to run, nausea, no appetite, breathlessness, racing mind, inability to hear, loss in concentration, numbness, pins and needles, and high levels of fear.

It can be difficult to explain to others the level of fear that you experience. All you know is that it is utterly horrible and you hope you never have a panic attack ever again. Problem number one!

Your mind is now on the lookout for an impending panic attack. This anticipation alone can make you feel anxious. This fear of having a panic attack releases adrenalin into the body. This in turn produces the symptoms of anxiety. If you then over-focus on these symptoms, you are at risk of having another panic attack.

Example:

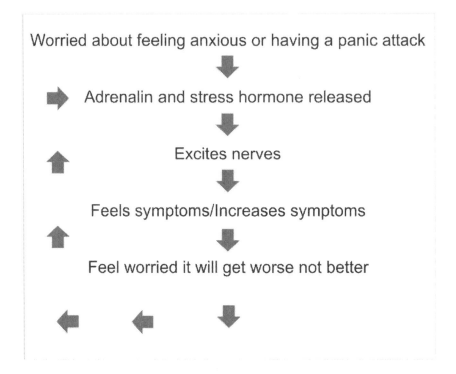

Worried about feeling anxious or having a panic attack

Adrenalin and stress hormone released

Excites nerves

Feels symptoms/Increases symptoms

Feel worried it will get worse not better

All the symptoms you feel are the result of adrenalin and will not harm you. You will not have a heart attack, you will not be sick and your legs will not give way etc. You are completely safe. Next time you feel ill from anxiety, you can remind yourself that it is just the adrenalin you can feel. It won't harm you and it will soon pass.

The symptoms of anxiety are actually your body's way of preparing itself to 'fight or flight'. We either decide to stay and fight or we run away. When we were cavemen our body's response to fear was very important to our survival. When faced with danger the body prepares itself for action. Whilst this was great for the cavemen it is not so great in our modern times.

So why does our body create such horrible symptoms? How can they possibly be helpful when under threat? Your legs shake because your body is preparing for your legs to start running. Your breathing speeds up because it helps your body prepare for muscular effort. You feel sick because the blood has been directed away from your stomach to your muscles to make them ready for action. You need the toilet because your body wants to be lighter and therefore faster. You might not notice this but your pupils will dilate in order to let more light in and enable you to survey the situation more accurately.

In a normal situation where there is a real danger, anxiety is a survival tactic to save us. If someone was chasing us, all the mechanisms of anxiety would provide us with a better chance of getting away. The muscles would work better and make us go faster. The problem with an anxiety disorder occurs when there is no real threat or danger.

When you experience panic attacks you normally remember where you were at the time. How could you forget? Problem number two! We mentally associate feeling bad to certain places or situations. One night I had a particularly bad panic attack round a friend's house. I had to wake my friend and phone my dad to ask him to come and pick me up. I felt humiliated and a complete failure. It was doubly unfortunate that my friend did not understand my anxiety.

The next week I tried to stay round another friend's house and I managed to cope. I think I coped because I was so determined. I did not stay round anyone else's house for a couple of months. When I did eventually arrange another sleep over I felt very anxious. I had forgotten about my success and remembered, extremely vividly, my failure. I failed again that night because I was so scared of failing. I did not stay round anybody else's house for a year. My mind had made the association that 'if I stay at a friend's house over night, I'll feel bad'. Thus every time I tried I was so anxious I had panic attacks and failed. This reinforced the belief.

Some people have increased anxiety in certain places. If an individual has had a panic attack in a shop, she may avoid that particular shop in future. She might even try to avoid all shops. She may get other people to go shopping with her or even get others to do her shopping for her. If an individual has a panic attack while driving a car, his solution may be to stop driving. Problem number three! They eventually avoid so many places it gets more and more limited where they can go. It can get to the point where they only feel safe in their own house. They become completely dependent on others. Even just the thought of going outside can result in a panic attack.

Avoidance is a short-term answer for not experiencing anxiety. It is a very poor long-term answer. The more you avoid your feared situation, the worse it becomes. The more you fear a situation, the harder it is to face that situation in the future.

Disturbing thoughts are the biggest reason panic attacks occur. They can stop you in your tracks. They can make you run home with your 'jelly legs'. They can give you horrendous panic attacks and make you avoid places, situations and even people.

Disturbing thoughts can come completely out of the blue. They can result from an over focus on the symptoms your anxiety is producing or they can appear when you are feeling completely fine. You might imagine a past event or perhaps a feared future event. It can almost be like a film running in your head.

You probably fight desperately to put these thoughts out of your head. You try so hard not to think about them but they still come. If I told you to not think of a pink elephant what do you think of? No doubt a pink elephant flicked into your mind. It is the same with disturbing thoughts. Trying to consciously not think of something is very difficult.

We often make our anxiety worse by adding more fear. There are two types of fear, First Fear and Second Fear. First fear is the fear which comes in the response to danger. Under normal circumstances we know that when the danger goes so will the feelings. For instance, imagine you are travelling in a car. The roads are icy and you hit a spot of black ice. The car slides and you lose control. Your car crashes into the car in front of you. You realise you are safe and unhurt. You feel the adrenaline in your body. You might feel like you have butterflies in your stomach. You might feel shaky and a little sweaty. You know that this is just an adrenaline rush and in a few minutes you will feel fine again. You dismiss it and what happens? The sensations go very quickly.

But what would happen if you were to concentrate and worry about your jelly legs, the nauseas feeling in your stomach, the shaky feint feeling, the fast heartbeat? Would those feelings lessen and pass as quickly? No. They would likely increase and intensify resulting in you feeling even worse. The sensations would take much longer to calm down and subside. This is because you added Second Fear.

First Fear could occur as a result of you thinking of an unsettling memory or a certain task that you need to carry out in the future. Alternatively, you might just suddenly feel anxious. First Fear may produce all the symptoms of the anxiety you know so well. Second Fear is the fear we add on top. In a sense you could look at it as First Fear being uninvited fear and Second Fear as invited fear.

You can easily recognise second fear. It is the fear you think about. It is the thoughts that start with 'what if'. It is the unpleasant pictures you put in your mind and re-think about over and over again. Let's imagine a young girl who suffers with anxiety. She decides to go to a nightclub. She arrives with a bunch of friends and sees a huge queue. She panics a little bit but manages to control it. Her and her friends join the queue. While they are chatting a huge wave of panic comes over her as she pictures herself feinting in the queue (First Fear). She could do one of two things. The first and most ideal reaction would be to relax and let the fear pass. She can ignore it and then engage herself in conversation. As a result of ignoring the First Fear, the fear would pass quickly and she

19

would be able to enter the club. She might still feel anxious but they would be feelings that she could manage. If she continued to ignore any first fear she experiences that night, the anxiety would begin to fade and she could enjoy clubbing. As she enjoyed her night and managed to cope with the little anxiety she had, she looks forward to going clubbing again.

Alternatively, whilst in the queue she might react to the First Fear with 'what if' thoughts. She might wonder 'what if I feint in front of all these people. Oh no. I feel really bad. I can't do this.' As a result she may experience increased anxiety or a panic attack. At this point she may decide she cannot cope and goes home. If she does manage to enter the club and still continues to have 'what if' thoughts, she may struggle with anxiety all night. She will likely feel that she cannot cope and decide to eventually go home. As a knock on effect, she may not wish to go night clubbing again as she thinks she will feel bad.

The best way to deal with First Fear is to relax. If you can accept that it is First Fear and it will pass quickly, you will experience success after success. You will begin to feel less anxious. You will recover from your anxiety and your panic attacks.

If you react to First Fear by adding Second Fear, you may find that you start to avoid certain situations and places. This can cause a negative spiral and you may be making your recovery longer. Adding second fear can add on weeks, months and even years to your recovery. It can cause you a huge amount of emotional distress.

Remember that First Fear is your body helping to keep you safe. Remember the cavemen and how the different sensations you experience are the body's way of preparing you to fight or run away. They can't hurt you. Remember the example of the car slipping on black ice and remember that the sensations of the initial fear will pass very quickly if you ignore them.

How We Feel

Isn't it strange how each time we experience anxiety, it feels different. You might think 'it's different this time. I really do feel ill. I couldn't possibly go out'. So you stay at home and what happens? You are completely fine! Try not to be fooled by any new sensation. Your anxiety is a clever little monster. It has so many tricks up its sleeve it is no wonder you think you are really ill. Whether you have a particular fear or phobia or are just scared of being outside and away from the safety of your own home, anxiety is completely terrifying. In a sense you have to distrust your own mind. Think of all the times you have felt like this or similar to this. How many times did you turn out to be actually ill? Chances are you have not. So chances are you will not be ill in the future. Take the risk and you will realise after about 1 hour, your feelings will settle down and you will feel better. If they don't you always have the option of returning home. Just try and see how you get on.

Anxiety can be difficult for people to understand if they have not suffered with it themselves. Although you might feel inclined to feel angry towards these people, try to appreciate that anxiety can be difficult to comprehend. It doesn't mean that people don't care about you. It just means they find it difficult to comprehend your illness.

I know you just wish they would listen to you. You want them to actually listen to what you are saying rather than just remaining silent while you speak. You may find that they are listening but their beliefs on your illness are so strong, it is difficult to change their mind. You might even find they start lecturing you about your illness and what you need to do to get better. People are generally just trying to help you. They think they can help by providing an outsiders perspective.

There are some amazing people in this world who can understand your anxiety even though they have not suffered with it themselves. They care for you, give you support and do not even mind all the cancellations. Whilst they might be supportive they can still find it difficult to fully comprehend with what you are going through. There will be odd times when you disagree. You might find you have a conversation with them that goes something like this:

'Why are you nervous?
'I can't help it. My body and mind are just a bit anxious.'
'But why? You have nothing to worry about.'

Depending on the situation you might try to explain your illness or you might decide to say something like 'I know but I can't help feeling anxious.' You might also decide to change the subject to take attention away from your illness. Try not to engage in an argument. It is understandable that even people who are the most supportive of you may find it hard to fully understand your illness.

Sometimes people will say things that can really upset you and knock your confidence. They probably think they are helping you. They might leave the conversation thinking 'I really helped her. I told her what I thought and how she can get better. I told her to just stop getting anxious. She was so ungrateful. She had a go at me! I don't know why I bother! She never listens to me.' It can be so frustrating.

Try to think back to that lovely time when you were well. Remember all those blissful days mucking about with your mates without a care in the world. What if instead of you, one of your mates developed what you have? Imagine they came to you and said, 'I can't come out tonight as I don't think I could do it. I'm too scared to go out clubbing. You might naturally ask why. You might then have the following conversation:

'I might feint.'
'Why would you? If you are worried, don't drink and you'll be fine.'

'No sorry. I can't. I am too anxious.'

'What? I don't understand. Please come. It's been arranged for ages.

'Sorry.'

Would you have understood? Would you have understood why your friend kept cancelling on you? Would it bother you? Would you listen and try to understand him? You may not have understood them either. I, to be honest, do not think I would. I would have probably thought the same as all the people who got on my nerves. I'm ashamed to say it and hope it would not have been my reaction. So any wonder these people do not understand you?

Guilt

Letting people down can make you feel so guilty. You might have to cancel arrangements, special events and holidays. Sometimes people may even try to make you feel guilty in the hope that you will change your mind and go.

You can't help your illness so why feel guilty of the impact it has on the people around you? You probably feel guilt because you are a sensitive, caring person and do not want to upset others. For instance, the anxious person who cancels on a friend often spends the whole night feeling bad. This is no good. You only put more pressure on yourself and prolong your recovery. Try to accept it has happened and what is done is done. Yes you may feel guilty but crying about it helps no one. It is best to take your mind off it by engaging yourself in an activity. It is not your fault. You might find you provide a large number of apologies. You might also find you tirelessly try to explain your illness. One sincere apology is enough.

Time Limits

When you feel guilty about letting others down, you may want to promise that you will be better soon 'I promise I'll be better by March'. This is most likely a desperate plea, hoping the person concerned will stick by you until then. Often time periods are unrealistic and promises are broken. Promising you will be well in a certain timeframe can ultimately increase the feelings of guilt that you experience if you do not achieve this goal. This can also lead to feelings of failure.

You might also give yourself time limits. You might think 'by next month I'll be able to do this and that.' If you do set yourself these time frames you can end up being disappointed when you do not achieve your goals. Rather than looking at what you have achieved, you may find that you focus on your failures instead. I realise you are desperate to get better. You probably feel that you have wasted so much time already. To stop yourself from feeling disappointed you must stop putting time limits on yourself.

Worried About Losing Loved Ones And Friends

The person suffering with anxiety can feel worried that they are going to lose their loved ones and friends. You believe everyone is annoyed with you and hates you for being ill. It can be a time when you find out who your friends are. The ones that stick by you are true friends. They will probably be your friends for life. If somebody does leave you, you must remember it is not your fault.

I met my previous partner at the time of being ill at 17 years old. I had been ill for 1 year, but on the mend. Unfortunately I became ill again because I stopped following the advice I was given. Throughout that time he stuck by me. I was also lucky that most of my friends never gave up on me. They kept me going. I did lose one friend. She did not understand my illness at all. We would argue and argue about it. Eventually we stopped getting in touch with each other. Years later we met up by chance and got friendly again. She is now one of my best friends and I can't imagine being without her. When I look back on this time, I realize that it wasn't really her fault that she didn't understand.

27

I was very lucky. I know some of you are probably finding it really difficult. I just hope there is at least one person you can rely on. It makes all the difference.

Dependency On Others

When you are anxious you may become more dependent on others. You may place demands on them and then feel angry when they turn you down. If they let you down you might take things more personally than you would normally.

You might also find you become more dependent on others as you will only go out if you have somebody with you.

Not Wanting To Be Left Alone

The thought of Monday morning and being on your own all week whilst everyone else is out at work can make you feel desperate. You might think 'What am I going to do? How will I cope with this week? I can't do it.'

If you are out, you may find yourself not wanting to return home as you'll be on your own again. You might choose to use the phone as much as you can. You may feel extremely lonely.

Wanting To Be How You Used To Be & How You Used To Feel

Why did I get like this? Why can't I be like my old self? I used to be happy, have fun and go on holidays. I was one of the gang! I wish it was like that again and I did not feel ill all the time. It's ruining my whole life.

Hoping For A Miracle In The Morning

See a shooting star and what would you truly wish for? If you found a genie in a lamp what would your three wishes be? I'll tell it to you straight. However hard you try, it is unlikely you will experience the miracle of waking up and not having anxiety ever again. Most people have to change their thought patterns in order to recover from anxiety.

Jealous Of Other People's Lives

It is easy to feel envious of anyone who has not got anxiety. But everybody has their own problems which weigh on their minds. Often people only allow you to see the positive parts of their lives.

Failures And Setbacks

Failures and setbacks are one of the most devastating things during recovery. You feel like you are doing really well. You think you are finally getting better. Then BOOM! It hits you like a ton of bricks. Something happens. Maybe it was a panic attack that sent you fleeing for your home or you were anticipating an event and got so anxious you could not get past putting on your coat. Failures can make you feel really low.

Sayings may go through your head like, 'I'll never get better. It's taking too long to recover. I've failed again. People think I am stupid. I try so hard, yet I get nowhere. That's it! I give up!' The incredible sadness you feel is unreal. However, as you begin to get better, going out becomes easier and failure becomes easier to handle too. You realize fretting about it gets you nowhere. Failures and setbacks are a normal part of recovery and you will be back on your feet within days.

Managing Anxiety Symptoms

I found that having a snack either before I went out or whilst I was out really helped my anxiety symptoms. I found bananas particularly good for this as they are very easy to eat. They raise your blood sugar which helps to stop you feeling feint and shaky. They are also great at settling your stomach.

Sometimes eating out can be really difficult if you are anxious. If you find swallowing difficult at times then go and grab something to eat right now. Now take your food, take a bite and chew it. Do not try to swallow. You will notice that eventually the food will disappear. Keep this knowledge with you at all times. You will be able to swallow your food. It might just take you a little longer.

When I was anxious I would also always have a bottle of water with me. Taking small sips helped to calm my nerves and settle my stomach.

If you don't have any food or drink with you, try taking a short rest. Sit down somewhere quiet for 10 minutes and you will find it can really settle your nerves. If you can, listen to some music, engage in conversation or just people watch.

You may have heard the advice to take some deep breaths. You can try breathing in for 4 seconds and then breathing out for 4 seconds. This works for some people but for me it made me feel light headed. I only recently (at the age of 34) learnt a new deep breathing exercise which does not make me feel light headed. Try breathing in for 3 seconds and then out for 5 seconds.

If you feel like you can't breathe at all, don't worry. You can breathe. The brain has an automatic function in it that will not allow you stop breathing. Think of when you hold your breath to stop your hiccups. At some point you suddenly gasp for air. Your brain won't let you stop breathing when you have a panic attack.

Medication

You may need medication in the early stages of recovery. It can be very helpful when you start counselling or for those first couple of months when you start to go out and face your fears. Anti-anxiety tablets are fast acting. They usually they take effect in 15-20 minutes. Tablets can help to reduce the anticipation of an event which may cause anxiety. They can also help to calm panic attacks. Your doctor will talk you through how your particular medication can help you and how long it takes for it to start working.

Anti-anxiety tablets can provide you with temporary relief but they are not a cure. They do not treat the underlying cause of the anxiety.

Some GP's will be very keen to prescribe anti-anxiety tablets and others may be less keen. If you feel medication would help you and your current doctor refuses to give you a prescription, try seeing a different GP. If you have a counsellor talk to him/her to see if they think anti-anxiety tablets would help you.

There are different types of anti-anxiety medication and different dosages. Your GP will decide which medication would be best for you. If you also feel depressed as a result of your anxiety your GP might suggest you use an anti-depressant to help lift your mood, whilst you work on your recovery.

If you do decide to take anti-anxiety medication, you may still feel slightly anxious at times. To ensure a full recovery it is important to still work on changing your thought patterns. Otherwise once you stop the medication your anxiety may return.

Counselling

Counselling can be extremely beneficial. When I had counselling I found it was really nice to be able to talk about how my illness was affecting me. Having somebody who would listen and understand was very therapeutic. I found sometimes when talking about my illness to family and friends, they would perhaps say things that weren't very helpful. The counsellor always made me feel better.

The counsellor will help you to identify the cause of your anxiety, if they deem this would be beneficial to you. They can also help to identify the next steps for your recovery. The counsellor will help you to choose small attainable goals and provide you with the strategies to achieve them. If you try to achieve one of your goals and fail, they will help you to unpick your thought patterns and identify what you could change. This will then hopefully lead you to achieving your goal in the future.

Some of you may think, 'I don't need a counsellor. My friends would laugh at me. Anyway, they are for other people, not me' Well that is your choice. No one can make you go. I will just say that a counsellor could help you get better quicker.

In 2014, the British Association for Counselling and Psychotherapy carried out some research on attitudes towards counselling. They found that 28% of people had consulted a counsellor or psychotherapist (up from 21% in 2010). The research reported that 54% of people said that they, a work colleague or a family member had consulted a counsellor or psychotherapist.

You can find a counsellor through your GP. You might be able to receive free counselling from NHS. They will be able to tell you what is available locally. About 50% of GP surgeries now offer talking therapies. If counselling is not available at your surgery they can refer you to a local counsellor. Depending on your surgery and your individual case, there may be a long waiting list. It can take months to be seen by a counsellor on the NHS.

If you can afford to pay for a counsellor privately, it will cost you between £30 and £100 an hour. You can ask your GP if they can recommend anyone locally.

Counselling can be delivered in a variety of ways. It can be face-to-face, online using Skype, by telephone or by email. If you suffer severely with anxiety you might find the online, telephone or email counselling preferable. You can often locate online, telephone or email counsellor through a web search engine. Ensure that you ask about the qualifications the counsellor holds. Some people will offer counselling and not have any qualifications.

There are different types of counsellor. They could be a Counsellor, Clinical Psychologist, Counselling Psychologist, Psychiatrist, Psychotherapist or a Cognitive Behavioural Psychotherapist.

You may find that you don't get on with your first counsellor. If that is the case, try another counsellor. It is important that you feel comfortable with your counsellor.

Hypnotherapy

Some people have the misconception that when you are hypnotized you have no control what so ever, the hypnotherapist can make you do anything and you are completely unaware of anything. This is not the case. The hypnotherapist lays you in a chair and talks calmly to your mind. They count you down into a state of deep relaxation. You are completely aware of everything being said and are completely in control of your actions. It just feels like that glorious feeling when you are really relaxed and are just about to drop off to sleep. That is all. If you wanted to, you could get out of your chair and walk out, although not advisable as you would be a bit sleepy!

Hypnotherapy works by relaxing your mind so the unconscious mind's barrier drops down. You can either use it to regress (go back to certain times) so you can deal with them or to put positive suggestions in your mind. Hypnotherapy has cured many people of anxiety.

Personally, I suggest you try counselling first and if that does not seem to be helping after 3 or 4 months perhaps try hypnotherapy. However, it is completely up to you.

Hypnotherapy is fairly expensive. However you will likely need fewer hypnotherapy sessions than counselling sessions. Some hypnotherapists claim they can cure you in as little as three sessions. But as with counselling it can depend on the individual as to how many sessions you will need.

I tried hypnotherapy and found it helped it a little. Personally for me counselling was far more effective. It depends on the individual.

Acupuncture

During my recovery I decided to try acupuncture. At the time I didn't really think it would work but decided to give it a go just in case.

I went to see a local acupuncturist who said that he could help me with my anxiety. I was nervous about the needles, but he told me they didn't really hurt.

The very fine needles go into certain points of the body that relate directly to anxiety. I had needles in my arms, legs, feet and stomach. I would then lie with my eyes closed with the needles in me. It sounds strange, but it was so relaxing. Afterwards I felt like I had had a deep refreshing sleep.

Acupuncture costs between £30 and £60 a session. I had about 10 sessions. You can ask your GP if he can recommend an acupuncturist.

If you can only afford to do one thing, I would try counselling. But if you can afford acupuncture too, it might be worth a try.

Worrying

Worrying is completely unproductive.

A good way to deal with worries is to ask 'Will this matter in a couple of months time?' For example let's imagine you are running late and stressing out or you have let somebody down. The chances are this will all be forgotten in a few months. If this is the case, try to relax a little and remember it's not really anything major.

There are steps you can do to minimize worry: Answer the following questions on a scale of 1 to 10. (1 = Definitely No, 10 = Definitely Yes)

Is it really likely to happen/to have happened?

Is any information that you have unreliable?

Is there anything you can do to stop your worry from happening or lessening the impact? How?

Are the consequences serious or life changing?

Try to put your worries in perspective. It always seems we have one major worry then if something bigger comes along that worry is completely out or the window or not as important. The bigger worry takes its place.

Worries often originate from irrational thinking. See if any of the below apply to you:

Everybody must think I am a nice person.

I must always be happy.

I must be loved and even adored by everybody that I ever meet.

I will only be liked if I continually please everybody.

If somebody does not like me, even at times, that means I must be a bad person and a failure.

I must be perfect in everything that I do otherwise I have failed.

I have no control over how I feel or what I experience.

I focus on mistakes, ignoring successes or saying they do not count.

I generalize things. For example, 'Because he finished with me that means every bloke I go out with will eventually do the same. I am a failure at relationships. Nobody will ever want to marry me.'

I can read people's thoughts and feelings to a tee. I believe because they said X, it means they think Y.

I believe everything will go wrong before I even attempt to take on the challenge.

I either magnify problems to make them into a huge thing or I ignore them and refuse to face them.

I believe thinking negatively about everything gives me an objective, more realistic view.

I believe everything should turn out exactly the way I thought or hoped it would. When it does not I become depressed and agitated instead of accepting it.

I hold myself responsible for events that are out of my control.

I assume people must behave in a certain way in order to make me feel good.

Criticism

Criticism can cause stress and anxiety. Ask yourself these questions:

Do I respect them?

Do they know more about this than I do?

Is their criticism reasonable?

Did they intend to try and help you?

Is it realistic?

Was it something that happened once but they said it always happens?

Was the criticism relevant to what you were talking about?

Is their criticism rational?

This should help you to put things into perspective and either take on board what the person said or completely dismiss it. Certain criticism, for example, when your boss flags up something they believed you could have done better, can actually improve your skills and coping strategies.

Failing

When suffering with anxiety you might regularly feel like you have failed. Ask yourself 'What would a friend's advice be to you? What advice would you give to a friend in your position?' You might like to remind yourself that this time you failed or made a mistake, but usually you enjoy success. Reflect on what you did right as well as wrong. Learn from it.

Problems

Next we are going to try to sort some of your problems out. We may not be able to sort all of them but at least by sorting a few of them some of the weight will be lifted off your mind. In some cases expert help may be needed i.e. when you are coping with a disturbing event. It may also be helpful to seek counselling for your problems, especially ones where you can see no way out. I would recommend counselling to anyone with anxiety but until you can afford it, receive your referral from the NHS, or if you do not want to go, then this chapter will be very beneficial to you.

Do the following exercise when you have a good 1 ½ hrs to spare. Sit somewhere on your own in a quiet room where you will not be disturbed. It needs to be a place where you feel calm and relaxed. You will need a pen and some paper. Next I want you to write down all your problems, every last little one. Then follow the instructions very carefully that I have written below. We are going to code your problems in severity.

1. Put a star next to every problem you think is quite easily solved.

2. Now put circles next to ones which are difficult but you think they can be solved i.e. you will hopefully not be stuck with them for life. Write them down, no matter how painful, embarrassing and difficult they will be to solve.

3. Next underline the ones which are completely not solvable such as turning 20 or bringing a person or animal back to life.

We are going to start with the problems marked with a **star**. On a new piece of paper write one problem at the top of the page and carry on writing each problem at the top of the page until they are all done. Now follow these instructions:

1. Think very hard, take your time and write down any possible solutions. Leave an inch between each one. Even if you do not think you would have the guts to carry it through or it sounds crazy still write it down.

2. Read each one and imagine carrying each one through. Write under each solution things which could go wrong, the pros and cons, and a rating out of ten as to how good you

think this solution is. Only do this if you think it is necessary to your particular problem.

3. Read through all the possible solutions to your problem. Judge each one on its effectiveness and put lines through all the solutions you think are not much good.

4. If you have a decision between a few solutions, it may help you to actually close your eyes and imagine the people and their personalities (if people are involved). If it is something you have got to say, say it out loud and in different tones of voice. Try to think when might be an appropriate time to speak to that person.

If your problem is not to do with anyone and is more of a personal problem maybe you could try a few solutions. Decide how much time you will give each one, bearing in mind you might not see a difference instantly. However, if one of your solutions is failing miserably then change it immediately. If your problem is an embarrassing medical problem it is very important you go to the doctors or chemist. They have seen it millions of times before. They are professionals. Remember, they do not know you. If they do know you and you are worried about it, go to a different doctor or chemist for this particular problem. If it is a sex problem which you may believe could be psychological then it may be helpful to talk to a counsellor. If you are too ashamed there are always telephone counsellors or online counsellors. Do not be afraid.

Next we are going to deal with the problems which are underlined. These are the problems that you cannot solve i.e. you cannot change them. To deal with these problems you need to find different ways of looking at them. For example, if you think you are not happy with your looks, write down all the things you like about yourself and all the things you think are okay. Next write down all the things that you do not have that you would hate to have. By doing this you will begin to realise how lucky you actually are. Also remember you cannot change it and worrying about it does not help, does it? No. It will just keep causing you stress and may make your recovery longer and we do not want that, do we? No. I know it is hard not to worry about it, especially when friends or family think it is funny to take the juice. Try to ignore them. A makeover is a good idea to boost your confidence or a new haircut.

If you are worried about turning a certain age, you can try to look at it from a more positive viewpoint. Think how long you have lived and the first five years you cannot remember much anyway. Also think how lucky you are, some people do not even make it to your age.

If your problem is that someone has died, it is important first of all that you grieve. This book does not go into detail about bereavement, so I suggest you read a special book on coping with bereavement if you think it may help. Professional help may also be of use to you. I know you probably think nothing will take your pain away and you are right it will not but it can give you ways to cope better. A nice way to remember someone or an animal is to make a scrap book of their life so you can remember the happy moments you both shared. Another positive thought is feeling privileged to have known them. You had the honour of sharing some of your life with them. You may want to plant a tree or flower in their memory. Remember they are always there in your memory.

If you have a serious illness counselling may help you cope.

There may be some problems which you had underlined which are now not as final as you first thought, however they do still seem difficult to solve. Mark these problems with an 'X'.

We are now going to move on to the problems marked with a circle. These are ones which are difficult, but possible, to solve i.e. they will not be here forever especially if we do something about them. I will warn you now these can be quite tricky to do.

1. Write each problem at the top of a new page as you did before.

2. Next to each problem on a scale of 1 to 10 (1 being least to 10 being max) rate how bad you consider it to be and how much it upsets you. Write just one number for each problem. We are going to deal with the easiest (lowest rated) first and work our way up.

3. Starting with your easiest problem (lowest rated) first, write down all the possible solutions for each one. Even if you think you could not do it, write it down.

4. Think really hard about each solution. Imagine carrying it out. How do you feel? How does it go? Write next to each how easily you would find it to carry out the solution. Use a scale of 1 to 10 (1 being very difficult 10 being fairly easy).

5. For each problem try the solutions which have the highest ratings.

Now to the problems marked with an 'X'. These are the hardest to solve, they are probably embarrassing problems or ones which you cannot face. I know it is hard. It may be leaving a dead end relationship and being scared to be on your own. You only have one life and if you are feeling stressed because of this problem then you have to break free. What is a few months of feeling hurt when you have freed your life up?

Your problem may be sex related and you are too embarrassed to seek help. Usually you know what to do about these problems. You need to go to the doctors, end that relationship, etc. If you feel you do not have the courage, then preparation is key. For example if you want to leave a relationship but you have kids and you feel can't leave, you may find reading relationship self-help books useful. You might decide to have counselling or seek professional advice. Emotionally prepare yourself. Work out what you will say to the people involved. Work out what you will do once you have told them. Work out what you will do to cope with your life in the immediate weeks or months afterwards. You might find absorbing yourself in socialising or a new hobby can help in this difficult time. Accept you might feel more emotional during this time.

Hopefully you now have some solutions or at least some ideas for how you are going to solve your problems that may be contributing to your depression. So start today and try some of these solutions.

You have done really well. Sorting out your problems is a big and difficult step and you are already half way there. Whatever you do, do not dismiss what you have just done. Do not put it to the back of a drawer and go back to your 'old ways'. If you still have problems you cannot solve, seek professional help.

A Day In The Life Of A Nervously Ill Person

Here is an example of a day in the life of a nervously ill person. You may identify with some or all of her feelings.

Jasmine is a 22 year old woman. She lives with her boyfriend, Jack, who is also 22 years old. They moved in together 3 years ago. Shortly afterwards Jasmine went on holiday and returned feeling ill. The pressure is taking its toll on their relationship and Jasmine fears the worst.

Jasmine wakes in the early hours of the morning, she turns over under her duvet and squints at the clock, 'Oh! It's only 4 am. Oh no! I've woken up early. Uh! That means I must be ill. (1). Jack goes to work in 2 hours. How will I cope? I'll have to make him stay off work.' Her panic mounts (2). She squeezes her eyes shut in the desperate hope something makes her fall asleep. Time passes and she holds her body tense fighting to fall asleep. 'Please fall asleep. Please fall asleep.' She chants in her head (3). Unsurprisingly this does not work. She rolls over and looks at her fiancée who is fast asleep. She wants to wake him. She feels she needs to wake him. She feels guilty (4). Deep down she knows what Jacks' response is going to be. She knows he will moan he has to get up soon and needs his sleep. He will be angry and absolutely no good to her. It will probably stress her out even more and make her feel worse (5). Jasmine knows all this but she still feels a compulsion to wake him. She hopes he will make her feel better. As she wakes him, he rolls over and murmurs. She prods him and Jack opens his eyes. He is facing the other way but he knows what is going to come next.

'I feel ill.'

'You'll be alright.' He rolls over, gives her a hug and drops off to sleep. Jasmine pushes him and says 'Wake up!' (6). He tries to ignore her. He knows she will be okay. Jasmine rolls over and huffs. She hopes demonstrating her annoyance at him will make him apologize and comfort her (7). When he does not comfort her, her tears start to form. While all this is going on she has forgotten her anxiety and the reason for waking him in the first place (8). She rolls over and looks at the clock and another pang of guilt hits her. Oh! She feels bad. She makes a point of turning over in her bed again hoping for some sort of communication. She wants Jack to comfort her and to stop her feeling guilty. She moves over to Jack. 'I'm sorry' she whispers (9) and pecks him on the cheek. No reply. She feels worse than ever. She feels agitated, annoyed and like her head is full of a jumble of thoughts (10). She rolls over and starts to think. She eventually drifts off and falls into a deep sleep (11).

Jack wakes up before the alarm goes off. He turns it off so it doesn't wake Jasmine. He goes to work (12).

Jasmine wakes and immediately looks at his pillow. She wonders where he has gone. She notices its light outside and checks the clock. She feels angry and says out loud 'Why didn't you wake me?' (13). She swears quietly but out loud to herself. She feels hurt. (14). Jasmine feels a number of emotions. She feels annoyed at her boyfriend. She looks at the door and sighs 'What a mess.' A slight wave of panic hits her as she bends down to get her slippers, deja-vu (15). She feels the same sadness most days. She sits upright and drags herself out of bed (16). Jasmine walks through into the kitchen and goes to the bread bin. She cooks her breakfast and slumps in front of the television. She forces (17) her breakfast down, mouthful by mouthful. Panic suddenly strikes as she remembers she has the doctors today. She carries on eating but the panic overcomes her and she gives up (18).

She sits in front of the television but nothing interests her. She is sulking. She re-thinks over this morning and her anger grows with Jack. She glances at the clock and thinks 'he has not even phoned me yet' (19). Jasmine decides to phone him. He seems okay on the phone but tells her he is going round his mate's house tonight. Jasmine takes this the wrong way and goes mad at him. 'Why are you going? Are you that mad with me you don't want to spend the evening with me?'

'You know that is not true. He asked me to help with some D.I.Y. at his house.'

'Didn't you think to ask me?'

'Well you said you wanted to stay in tonight.'

'Yeah, I wanted to stay in tonight with you!' She yells.

'Okay, I'm sorry. I won't go.'

This is what Jasmine really wants but she says 'No you go. I'll get a friend round. Urgh! You know I hate being on my own at night. Why Jack, why?'

'Sorry. Listen Jasmine, I don't mean to be rude but I am dying for the toilet. I'll call you later.'

'Do you want dinner?'

'Please.'(20).

The phone goes dead. She moves on to the couch again. She hates herself for being so possessive (21). After 5 minutes of thinking it all through, she calls him back and apologizes to him. Now she feels okay and can get on with her day (22).

She goes upstairs and has a shower (23). Feeling much better, she makes the bed and goes downstairs. Something catches her eye on T.V. and she sits down to watch it. It is a medicine documentary and as she watches it she feels slightly panicked. It is about a man who is fine when he woke in the morning but by 5pm that evening he passed out and was found the next day by the milkman collecting his wages (24). Jasmine immediately thinks it could happen to her.

She was going to see if she could make it to the shops this morning. She didn't need anything but thought it would be a challenge. She wanted to see if she could do it (25) but what if she was to feint while out? Her head buzzes with confusion. Is she feeling okay? 'Actually' she thinks 'I do feel ill (26). I can't go out. What about the doctors? Oh no and Jack is going out tonight. I've got no one. I will be on my own.' Jasmine gets more and more stressed at these thoughts.

Jasmine looks at the washing up and feels like she is not up to doing it. She then starts to fret that she won't be able to make Jack his dinner tonight and this will make him mad. She falls onto the sofa. How could this be happening to her she thinks, today of all days when she has to go to the doctors (27). She realizes she needs to calm down. (28) and goes to phone Jack. At the last moment she resists and calls her Mum instead. There is no answer so she tries to call her brother. Her brother was great on the phone. He listened to her and says she is fine. But, he sounded bored.

Jasmine decides to watch some more television and changes the channel. She can't stop thinking she feels ill. She concentrates on her stomach, then her head and by the end of the hour she feels physically ill. She thinks 'That's it! Someone will have to come round and look after me!' She tries to call her Mum and her mum answers this time. 'I'm really bad Mum. Will you come round?' (29).

'Sorry love. We are really busy here at work. I couldn't possibly get away. We have 2 people off sick.' Jasmine cries and then proceeds in phoning nearly everybody she knows and then finally Jack. She truly hates herself for it but asks him to come home. He says she can't expect him to drop everything for her. But the sad truth is that she does (30).

Jasmine lies back on the sofa and manages to calm down but her mind begins to think again. She wonders about the two people at her Mum's work who were ill. 'What were they ill with' she worries. She adds more panic but again manages to calm down. She feels rough still but the panic gets less and less. She feels shaken yet okay (31).

By now it is dreaded lunchtime. Preparing and then eating her food on her own is a chore (32). 'What if I have a panic attack during my lunch? How will I cope?' (33). It is as if everything she does in her day can cause her to panic from waking up to going out.

Lunch goes unexpectedly well. Jasmine washes up and then looks round the lounge. 'What could I do now?' Feelings of boredom, loneliness, tiredness and depression overcome her. The doctor appointment is in a couple of hours. She questions herself to see if she is well enough to go.

Jasmine looks round the house. The vacuuming needs to be done but she could not possibly do that because she gets panic attacks when she vacuums (34). Plus it would tire her out for the doctors. So she decides she had better rest. The only way she thinks she can rest is to watch television. She goes into the cupboard and picks out a movie that has been watched many times before. She watches it for 1½ hours accompanied by the occasional surge of panic. She concentrates on the panics for a while until she forgets and watches the movie again (35).

She feels okay and gets ready for the doctors. Hang on a minute! Oh no! She feels dizzy! She puts her coat on but then sits down due to her light-headedness (36). She realizes time is running out and decides she has to go now. She will prove to Jack she can do things (37). She steps outside. Wow! She feels bad but she forces herself. (38)

She is now a quarter of the way there and she realizes she has forgotten her anxiety pills (39) What if I have a panic attack?' She panics. Half way there and she is thinking, 'How will I cope?' The dreaded panic attack comes. She stands still, rooted to the spot. She fights it, all the time thinking, 'You are not going to beat me. (40). Ah! I feel bad but I can do it! I'll show Jack I am getting better.'

Jasmine eventually arrives at the doctors. Typical! It's busy, hot and extremely stuffy. She has serious thoughts about turning around but the receptionist asks her name. That's it! She is stuck. Jasmine takes a seat, trying not to breathe much as she does not want to catch someone else's germs. She panics and feels as if everybody is watching her. They would think she is really stupid if she just walked out (41).

She suddenly pictures herself just falling to the floor (42) and a huge panic attack comes this time. Her name is suddenly called, 'Jasmine Banks' and she stands up and goes into the room as fine as can be (43).

When she comes out she feels good and can even go and get her prescription (44). She arrives home and phones her friend up to ask if she can go round hers tonight. Her mate is really chuffed. She cooks dinner and feels the sweet taste of success. Yes. It is so sweet!

As she serves up dinner her energy begins to flag and she feels quite exhausted. Her mood drops and Jack walks in. Unfortunately she no longer feels up to seeing her friend but feels she must go. For half an hour she says 'I'm going, no I can' t. ' She gives up and plans what to say when she cancels (45).

The atmosphere in the house is very tense. Jasmine can feel her anxiety rising (46) as they sit down to eat their dinner. Jasmine is particularly uncomfortable and keeps having to stop to have panic attacks (47). She does not eat much as she has no appetite. Jack gets ready to go and see his mate. Desperation creeps in (48). Jasmine and Jack have the 'please stay in to look after me' conversation. Jack agrees but then Jasmine cannot cope with the guilt and tells him to go. He leaves the house and slams the door. Jasmine breaks down and cries, 'How could he? He doesn't love me.'

She immediately picks up the phone and calls her Mum and then her Dad. Both tell her they can't come round. She is on her own and feeling bad. She has a big panic attack so decides to phone Jack on his mobile but does not know what to say. Jack comes home. Jasmine feels so much guilt and believes he is going to leave her as he is really annoyed. She wishes she was just well. She's been ill for so long. She thinks hurry, hurry, get better Jasmine'. (49)

Jasmine now faces the task of phoning her friend. The butterflies in her stomach make it worse. She knows her friend will be mad and will not understand. She picks up the phone and dials.

'I'm sorry. I feel too ill to make it.'

'What's wrong with you?'

'I feel sick and dizzy.'

'Again?'

'I'm really sorry.'

'It's all in your head. Just forget it. Ignore it. Why don't you just trust me when I say you will be okay?'

'I feel anxious, I can't ignore it and I do trust you.'

'You're going to lose all your friends at this rate.'

Jasmine tries to explain. 'It is an illness. It takes time to get better.'

'Well call me when you are well. You've messed me about too much. Goodbye. (50)

The phone is slammed down. Jasmine slowly replaces the receiver. She bursts into tears and Jack sits her down. They talk. He makes her feel better by saying her friend is no friend whatsoever and she is better off without her. Jasmine only has a few friends (51) and her other 2 are brilliant. Jack then makes her feel worse by saying, 'You have to look at it from her point of view. Everyone gets stressed with you now and then' (52). Realizing what he has just said he desperately tries to apologize. Jasmine cries.

The atmosphere is awful in the house. They both stay in the night and watch T.V. At 9pm Jack announces he is off to bed. Jasmine stays up to try and 'sort herself out.' (53). She gets nowhere and reluctantly gets into bed. Jack is half asleep. She tries to get to sleep but cannot stop herself thinking about her life. There are so many problems. An hour passes and as she realizes the time. She tries to put these thoughts out of her head but finds it impossible. She feels so wide-awake her eyes will not even stay shut. She tosses and turns and eventually falls into a light sleep at 1.30am.

Explanations Of How Jasmine Felt and How She Could Have Helped Herself.

1. Jasmine thinks back to times when she has been ill and woken in the early hours. She should realize waking at odd times is perfectly natural. She may have woken due to a disturbing dream, a noise outside or simply because she has had enough sleep.
2. Jasmine adds second fear and creates her own panic.
3. How could she possibly sleep when she is holding herself so tense? She could try to relax her body and close her eyes. Resting with her eyes closed is nearly as beneficial as sleeping.
4. Guilt is one of the most common emotions when suffering from anxiety.
5. She knows how he will react but still feels she 'needs' to. Sometimes you may just need to feel the security of someone else being awake. Jasmine should try and resist as much as she can.
6. Jasmine feels dissatisfied at Jack's attempt to comfort her and so tries to gain his attention once again.
7. She needs comfort more than anything right now and cannot understand why he is being selfish in wanting to sleep. Jack knows she will be okay, she is not 'really ill' and it will pass so he does not think he needs to bother.

8. When you are suffering from anxiety, having something to concentrate on can help. If Jasmine could have realized her anxiety had gone, she could then have realized it was just anxiety.

9. You may find you apologise a lot when suffering with anxiety due to the guilt you feel. One apology is enough. If you keep apologizing the person may get annoyed.

10. You may feel you have too many thoughts in your head. You just want a 'clean' head. It feels messy due to agitation and confusion. You know what makes you feel worse, yet you carry on doing it. Try to write down what makes you feel worse such as constant apologies, phoning people up when you know they will be mad with you. I know sometimes you feel you 'have to' but try to be strong.

11. Now her attention has moved from her anxiety to other problems, she falls asleep.

12. Jack did this out of thoughtfulness.

13. Nervously ill people often take things the wrong way. If Jasmine took a minute and put herself in Jacks shoes she could understand why he did it i.e. so she could sleep. Considering another person's perspective can save a lot of resentment.

14. There is a lot of emotional pain to be felt during anxiety including pain of feeling unloved, pain of letting others down, pain of being ill etc.

15. Jasmine has been here so many times before that her mind links it to anxiety. If she moved her slippers or did not put any on it may break the cycle and she would feel much better.

16. She needs a more positive outlook. I know it is hard. She could put on some music, take a few deep breaths and stick her head out of the window. This would make her feel much more positive and she could therefore tackle the day with more ease.

17. Eat food slowly. Just keep chewing and eventually the food will disappear.

18. Jasmine could have let the panic pass and then carried on eating.

19. Anxiety can make you feel concerned that you have annoyed people and they have stopped loving you. This can produce feelings of anger towards the person. In addition, you might have less patience with people than you normally would.

20. Jasmine took it the wrong way. She thought the worst. It caused an argument. The problem lies in the fact she feels Jack no longer loves her. This makes her feel

clingy and more dependent on him. The abrupt ending to the phone call makes it worse.

21. She is not possessive but dependent on other people. Anybody who is ill is more likely to be dependent on others. Even Jack when he is ill with flu he is dependent on Jasmine. It is the same thing. Due to her feeling she is unloved she becomes more needy.

22. Once sorted, she feels okay.

23. A good therapy is to feel the water wash away the morning stresses.

24. She must realize this is a freak incident. Television shows about medicine are not a good idea if you are suffering from anxiety.

25. You should never 'test' yourself. Look at it as practice. She adds second fear and considers the 'what if's'.

26. Over concentrating on your body can make you perceive that you are not feeling well, even if you are feeling fine. Jasmine's muscles tense, adrenalin is released and she feels ill.

27. She has added second fear. Her best bet would have been to relax, take her mind off it and do something or think about something else.

28. Good!

29. She pleads not to be on her own.

30. Often the nervously ill person expects everybody to drop everything for them and to do absolutely anything for them. It can be upsetting when this is not possible.

31. Panic does not actually harm you. IT ALWAYS, ALWAYS CALMS DOWN. After suffering a severe panic attack you may feel a bit shaken but this will pass in approximately half an hour.

32. Many things are a chore. Thinking about them is usually worse than actually doing them.

33. Jasmine is not scared of her original fear, now she fears fear itself. This releases adrenalin and produces exactly the symptoms she fears.

34. Jasmine fears using the vacuum as she had a panic attack once when using it. She has now associated the two. The other reason she may feel anxious while vacuuming is due to the exertion because she shallow breathes. She then mistakes this for the beginnings of a panic attack.

35. T.V. is not really a good form of rest before you go out, unless it is truly interesting. Otherwise your mind is not fully occupied and panic will keep coming. A better idea would be to read a book, magazine, do some drawing etc. In the 30 minutes before you go out you can try spending time deciding what to wear, doing your make-

up or styling your hair. This helps to take your mind off your anxiety just before you have to go.

36. She makes an issue out of it. If she said, 'Okay. I feel dizzy. But then I knew I would. I have not felt dizzy all day and I do now I have to go out. Therefore it must be anxiety. Anxiety cannot harm me. I am safe.'

37. Having an incentive can be very beneficial to your recovery but do not put excess pressure on yourself.

38. You might feel anxious when you first step outside. This is normal. Remember if you do feel anxious don't add second fear and the feelings will pass quickly.

39. Realizing you do not have your pills can alone bring panic.

40. She fights when she should float. I will show you how to 'float' later in this book.

41. In fact they would not. They may think she is going to her car to get something, going to use her mobile phone or just needs some air. No one would care. People are normally too wrapped up in their own thoughts in a doctors surgery to be thinking about others.

42. Thoughts like this are unstoppable. When they come, realize they won't happen. They never have. It is JUST anxiety.

43. As soon as the situation changes and she will be safe with the doctor, the panic disappears.

44. Once you can go home you often feel you can do more.

45. She feels bad and debates what she should do. She is suffering from anticipation. If she said I'll just go for ½ an hour she could make it and probably stay longer.

46. When you are stressed, worried or tense you may find you become more anxious.

47. This is due to the stress she is feeling. She needs to just take her time.

48. Any ill person is dependent on others to some degree.

49. The anxious person may frequently beg not to be alone and then feel guilty they have ruined other peoples' plans. Try to keep as strong as possible. Jasmine says, 'Hurry! Hurry! Hurry!' as she has been ill for so long and she realizes it is putting pressure on her relationship. She has to accept it takes time and try to remain as strong as possible.

50. It is virtually impossible to explain to a friend who does not want to understand. They think they already understand your illness.

51. Anxiety is a crippler for anybody's social life. Do not take it personally.

52. You may realize this but you do not need people to tell you it. Remember, you get stressed with others and

others get stressed with others. So where is the difference?

53. This barely works for the anxious person, especially at night. She is best to cut her loses and get some rest. In the morning she will feel better.

How To Cope When You Have A Panic Attack

We have talked about what causes panic attacks so we know how we can minimize them. However, we still need to know how to cope with them when they do come. When we experience a panic attack everything else around us seems to disappear. We are in our own little world and all our awareness is focused on how we feel.

The most common way in which people deal with something that is terrifying or makes them feel uncomfortable, is to either 'run away' or ' fight' it. With panic attacks neither works. If you use the avoidance tactic of running away, there becomes less and less places you can go until you are eventually housebound. The fighting tactic may get you through it but by gritting your teeth, holding your body tense and yelling inside your head 'I'm not going to let you beat me', you put yourself through so much emotional and physical torture it is less than ideal.

Floating Through Panic Attacks

You can float, pass through the panic attack and let go. By doing this we relax our body. No or very little adrenalin is released. Physical symptoms lessen/disappear and we can carry on with whatever we were doing. It reinforces the truth that panic cannot harm you and it always calms down.

You will experience success after success and therefore recover as quickly as possible. When you first practice floating it can feel slightly scary. Once practiced a couple of times you realize you are safe and it does calm the panic attack.

It is hard to float to begin with. First you need to physically relax your shoulders. Imagine you have a string on each shoulder and someone is sitting below you and pulling the string down in order to bring your shoulders down. Physically pull them down.

You may find a visual technique can help you float. You may like to use one of the below or make one up of your own. Imagine:

- You are on a bus, the panic attack is a big cloud of black smoke that you are PASSING THROUGH at a constant speed and come out of the other side (when the panic attack calms down).

- You are sitting on a cloud. You hit the attack, GLIDE THROUGH IT and come out the other side (once it has calmed down).

- You are on roller skates and you WHEEL THROUGH the fog and come out the other side (once it has calmed down).

- You are in a swimming pool. Swim slowly through the panic attack.

As you are walking along and you actually get your panic attack, imagine that you are just walking through a bad patch in the air.

Try to think of some of your own and use whichever one makes you feel the most comfortable and safest.

When you first begin to use the floating technique you may feel anxious to begin with. Persevere and with practice you will see how much easier it is to cope.

It does take a lot of courage to let go. Practice makes perfect.

Calming A Panic Attack

1. Realize it for what it is. A panic attack and it cannot harm you. You are safe.

73

2. Relax your shoulders and face if you can. Use a floating technique. Do not worry how long it takes, it does not matter. Concentrate on floating and the relaxation of floating.
3. DO NOT ADD ANY SECOND FEAR.
4. Remember it is just a panic attack.
5. Once the panic has calmed down enough for you to do your deep breathing, do it.
6. Expect to feel a little shaken! Don't let it worry you. It is not important.
7. Pat yourself on the back. You did not let the little devil scare you.

Please note: This is the correct way to recover from anxiety. It will take time to get it right but once you do, it will be like second nature. Do not stress if you 'slip up' occasionally or a lot in the beginning! Practice makes perfect. You will get there.

Second fear - It is important you try not to add second fear. It can be tempting when you are trying to float to think, 'If I relax all the things I fear, such as physical illness, will happen. What if XYZ happens?' In fact the complete opposite will happen – nothing will happen! Try it for yourself. Knowing you are safe and panic holds no fear, the 'little devil' has no control over you and you can go out as panic attacks no longer scare you. You have the cure now!

Under Pressured And Over Pressured

During your recovery you will experience different stages. There will be moments when you suddenly realize you have no anxiety. Some weeks you may find it is harder to go out than other weeks. There will be times when you feel you have made real progress and times when you feel nothing in the world could stop you.

In this chapter I will talk to you about realizing your achievements and how to take off some of the pressure associated with going out.

Feel As If You Are Not Achieving?

As you recover you may forget exactly what you have achieved and do not see the point in carrying on. To really realize how much better you are, take an A4 piece of paper. Now think back to the time when you were at your worst. Maybe you were housebound. Start at the beginning and write down every little achievement you have made to date. You will realize just how well you HAVE done. Continue to add to it every time you achieve something. It can be useful to refer to this list if you experience a setback and feel you are getting nowhere.

Can't Be Bothered?

There may be times when you would like to do something but simply cannot be bothered to cope with the anxiety. Personally I loved clubbing before I became ill. There would be times when I was anxious, yet still felt I could manage it but would not go as I did not want the hassle of the anxiety. To feel this way is quite understandable. Anxiety is painful, it makes you feel physically ill, it is terrifying and it can walk all over a good time. In this situation it really is up to you what you do. Sometimes you will feel you have enough energy, sometimes you will not. To occasionally not try and go out is okay but make sure you don't let it become a habit.

There will be periods in your recovery when you feel unenthusiastic about pushing yourself that little bit further. You get stuck in a rut and cannot be bothered to break free. There are a few tricks of the trade to get you out of this one.

Buy a new top for the event or as a reward.
Concentrate on the fun you could have.
Reward yourself once you have done it.
Just go for a short while.
Daydream scenarios for example maybe at the party you will meet a new partner.

Give yourself a new image so you can go and show it off! Wear a new skirt or have a new hairstyle.

Stuck In A Rut?

When you are well on the way to recovery you need to be aware of the certain stages you might pass through. These stages can trick you into feeling you have got this far and that is as far as it goes. You may get to a point where you can do everything that you need to in everyday life but you don't feel like you want to push yourself any further. Maybe you feel too scared to start a new job, go out for a whole day or stay at a friend's house for the night. You are capable of carrying out your daily tasks and feel quite happy.

Allow this phase for a while, while you recuperate. But you MUST, in order to make a full recovery, give yourself a hard push. Once you push yourself into the next phase you may find it difficult to begin with and suffer with more anxiety but do not go back. Keep on in there. It's just because it's new. After a couple of times of trying something, you realize, 'Hey! I didn't get too anxious then! It eventually gets like a well oiled cog and you are in the same position of not feeling anxious and feeling comfortable most of the time, yet one stage up. You can have a rest in the comfort zone and then give yourself a hard push into the next stage. The stages get quicker and quicker, easier and easier and you end up fully recovered.

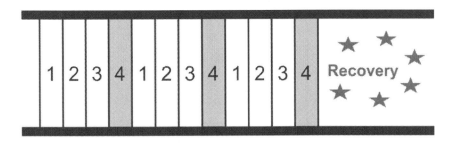

KEY

1 – Difficult. Need to push yourself.

2 – Easier

3 – Easy

4 – Comfort zone

Sometimes people feel cheated when they finally pluck up the courage to try an activity they have been dreading and find they have no or little anxiety. The lesson to be learnt here is, THINKING ABOUT DOING IS OFTEN WORSE THAN THE ACTUAL DOING.

Out Of Your Depth?

Only EVER do what you feel capable of doing. It does not matter how long you have been ill or how quick you want to get better. You cannot hurry recovery. You can help to shorten it by practicing what your counsellor and I teach. If you hurry it and put excess pressure on yourself, your recovery may be longer. Only ever do what YOU feel you can do. Do not allow yourself to be pressured into something you cannot do. If you do you are likely to experience failure and setback. This creates negative thought patterns and recovery will seem far off.

TIP: If you do manage to achieve something major, use it as a reference point for smaller tasks. If I managed to go up the city on my own then I can manage to walk to the local shop on my own.

Feel You Have Too Much Planned?

Look at your diary or write down everything that you have to do.

Option 1
Ask yourself these questions to try and sort out your diary so you have less to do.

Is there anything which I could completely cancel?

Is there anything I could do next week or another time?

Could I shorten the length of time it will take?

Could I combine two things in one?

P.S. Could you learn to say 'no'?

Option 2

Look after yourself. Eat well and exercise. De-stress and rest up between events. Take them one by one. Deal with each day as it comes rather than looking at the whole week.

TIP: To make yourself less anxious it can be a good idea to always take a bag with you. In it can be any tablets you may need e.g. indigestion, anxiety pills, bottle of water, food, mobile phone or money for a payphone if you ever need to be collected, telephone numbers, this book or a note book on how to cope and something to take your mind off the anxiety maybe a magazine, cards, music or phone/tablet.

My phobia was of being sick while out. So I always carried a carrier bag with me in case I was sick. Is there anything you could take with you to give you more security?

Forgotten How To Cope

There are two ways you can overcome this problem. You can re-read this book constantly. Read a chapter a week, or write down all the things which you want to remember and then write them on pieces of paper and put them on the wall. By doing this these positive messages are going into your mind all the time. It really, really helps and I believe it helped my recovery enormously.

Things you could write are:

Panic always disappears.

Panic does not actually harm you. It always calms down

You will not actually be ill

You CAN do it

Float

You are safe

You could draw yourself a diagram of how to cope with a panic attack.

You could go through this book and pick out other things you may find useful.

Self-Nurturance

If you have been working really hard on your recovery, give yourself permission to take a couple of days off. Just spend the time chilling out and having a rest. It will leave you brimming with energy ready for your next ventures out of the house.

Bad Days

Bad days are not just bad they are terrible, aren't they? I am sure you are the first to agree. They rob you of everything you have going for you, your ambition, well-being, confidence, energy, health and they especially rob you of thoughts of recovery.

On a bad day your thoughts may consist of 'I'll never get better. I'm useless. Everyone may as well give up on me, I can't ever go anywhere, I am a freak' etc. You might experience panic attacks or just feel generally ill.

Good days are not just good, they are fantastic! You feel you could conquer the world, nothing stands in your way, you feel amazing and you know, as you should do, you are going to get better.

When you are in the depths of suffering an anxiety disorder, the bad days well out way the good. You may hardly ever have a good day. Then you will get them occasionally, then twice a week, then more, until you hardly ever get bad days.

Bad days will happen whether you like it or not. There is no way of stopping them. The way to cope with them is to change the way we look at them. If we worry about them, they can literally feel unbearable. So how do we go about this?

Think of your recovery in yet again stages. When you experience a bad day or setback, take a couple of days out of your recovery program. These are REST days. These are days in which you can do whatever you like. Do not bother to go out or maybe just go out for a short walk if you like, but do not push yourself. I want you to do exactly what you like, laze in bed all day, watch videos, do your hobby, phone all your friends, pamper yourself, read a book, play games or anything else that you enjoy. Look at it as an opportunity to relax and gather your energy for the next stage. It will leave you feeling vibrant, confident and ready for the next hurdles. Realize and remember recovery cannot happen without set backs or bad days. It is a SYMPTOM of recovery. So it is not a bad thing. Accept. Accept. Accept!

In the beginning you may feel bad days mean a lot and you need to talk to someone, cry about them and shout about them. As you begin to recover you realize even though they are upsetting, you can accept them for what they are. You realize they are not important and worrying and stressing about them gets you nowhere. You can look upon them as a rest. You can do this because you know you will be back on your feet within a couple of days, because you always are. If you practice this you will be amazed at the difference it makes.

It can be beneficial, particularly in the beginning, to work out why you have experienced a bad day or setback in order to lessen the times it will happen again. It may have happened due to stress, fatigue, worrying about future events, unsolved problems, not eating properly or not looking after yourself, therapy 'coming out', adding second fear, there was too much for you to do/cope with or maybe it was something else. At times there will be no reason as to why it happened so do not worry if you cannot find the cause.

NO ACHIEVEMENTS ARE EVER, EVER LOST. WHATEVER HAPPENS THEY WILL ALWAYS BE WITH YOU AND NEVER DISAPPEAR.

Friends, Family and Events

Anxiety in itself is hard enough to cope with but the thing that can make it ten times worse is other people. In this world people can make you feel on top of the world or really low. However, they only have the power if we let them.

When it comes to anxiety, unless they have been there themselves or someone close to them has, it can be extremely hard for people to understand. There are people who want to listen and understand and people who think they already understand and therefore do not want to listen. In your life one group may out way the other whereas in somebody else's life it may be the opposite.

For the people who do not understand but want to, you must be 100% honest. Tell them how you feel, tell them how you are going to get better, what your body does when you have a panic attack, what they should do, how they can help, what makes you feel bad and good, your capabilities and most important of all tell them how much you appreciate them listening and giving you their support. These people are very important in your life right now. If you feel like you cannot see them as arranged, tell them it is the anxiety. Don't make any fake excuses. If they find out you have lied, they will lose respect. Sometimes these people might say the occasional comment which frustrates you such as 'can't you come with us yet? When will you be well?' They mean no harm. Do not be upset by any of it.

Occasionally a person who you thought understood suddenly has a problem with it. You will probably feel angry at them and it can be more upsetting than somebody who never understood. You cannot see why they were so brilliant in the beginning and now are the worst of the lot. Unfortunately I cannot give you an answer to why this sudden change occurs. It may be due to stress or impatience. It might be that in the beginning they thought you were ill and thought something could physically happen to you. Now they know that nothing happens to you and you are safe, they can't understand why you get scared. You can try asking them for their reasons. You may get an answer to which you can explain the situation. They may then understand or they may not.

The people who don't understand are frustrating and annoying. They can make you feel really low. Now you will be shocked but I am going to stick up for these people. Yes I agree they do all of the above and much more besides but here it comes, it is not their fault. To put this point across I want you to understand them. Isn't that want you want them to do for you? So you can make the first effort.

I want you to imagine you are in a room and having a very heated argument with a friend. Imagine the madness, tension and anger that you would feel. In this argument you are wrong, but you think you are right. You are having the argument and you do not want to hear the other person's point of view. You think you are right, you give your opinions and you like the sound of your own voice. At times you might be quiet and pretend to be listening, but your mind is mind up.

It's the same with the anxiety. The people who don't understand think they are right. They do not think they could be wrong so they do not listen to what you say. Arguing with them is pointless.

Now you understand why they are like they are, they should be easier to cope with. The things they say to you will still hurt, upset and irritate you, so we need to find a better way of dealing with them. You know explaining your illness to them does not work. Their statements are not true. They know nothing about it, they cannot judge you. Ignore them and put it down to misunderstanding. Do not let these people get to you.

If you have to cancel on these people:

1. BE STRONG.

2. Get straight to the point. 'I will not be coming round because I am too anxious. Sorry to have cancelled on you, maybe another time. Do not arrange when. Try to only apologize once. Do not apologise more than twice.

3. Either carry on the conversation or end it.

4. It they start getting at you, firmly say, 'There is no point in me trying to explain my illness as you will not understand. So let's just leave it yeah? I don't want to argue with you.' You have to be firm and strong. There is no other way. You can do it.

Try not to let others slow your recovery.

Special Events

These are difficult. Tell the person who has invited you how much you would like to go. Thank them for the invite and say you will try your hardest to make it. You can say this to people who understand and people who don't understand your illness. If the person is annoyed then at least they are annoyed with you today rather than being annoyed with you on their special day.

Holidays

When you are away from home it can be tempting to go back to your old ways. You might be tempted to try and fight the panic attack or add second fear. This is because you are feeling anxious and unsure. It you revert back to your old ways, you will feel worse. Wherever you are in the world, and whatever you are doing, the same rules always, always apply. Your tool box of cures will always work.

Holidays can be difficult as the pressure to go can be immense. The money has already been paid, time has been booked off work and your partner/family/friends constantly enquire whether you will up to it. You might find that you keep saying you will be fine, but deep down you are not sure that you will be. The hardest thing about going on holiday is probably the anticipation. The indecisiveness of should you go, shouldn't you go. If you can withstand the anticipation and the first few days of the holiday, the rest will be easy. You take your real home with you, your partner, family or friends. You feel safe with these people. You are safe. Good luck! When you come back you might experience slight anxiety at going back into your old routines. It will soon pass.

Good Things That Come Out Of Anxiety

If we go through any trying experience in life we are bound to learn something from it. Once you have successfully beaten your anxiety, some of the things you will have learnt are listed below. There will be more than those listed as some of the learning will be personal to you.

You become more understanding towards others illnesses and problems.

You learn how to relax and deal with stress.

You sort out who your real friends are and they will probably be friends for life.

You become a stronger and better person.

You become a good listener.

You realize if you can get through an anxiety disorder you can cope with anything life chooses to throw at you.

You can cope with shocks by using the same techniques.

Improved diet and exercise regime.

When you need to face normal nerve racking situations such as job interviews you can handle your nerves better than most.

You know if you try hard at most things you will succeed.

Printed in Great Britain
by Amazon.co.uk, Ltd.,
Marston Gate.